For Glen (aka Poppy G.), who is always willing to dive in —S. M.

For Katie, Benny, and George —D. L.

For glaciers—stay chill —O.

Henry Holt and Company, *Publishers since 1866*

Henry Holt® is a registered trademark of Macmillan Publishing Group, LLC

120 Broadway, New York, NY 10271 • mackids.com

Text copyright © 2020 by Stacy McAnulty

Illustrations copyright © 2020 by David Litchfield

ISBN 978-1-250-10809-8

Library of Congress Control Number 2019940943

Our books may be purchased in bulk for promotional, educational, or business use. Please contact your local bookseller or the Macmillan Corporate
and Premium Sales Department at (800) 221-7945 ext. 5442 or by email at MacmillanSpecialMarkets@macmillan.com.

First edition, 2020 / Designed by Sophie Erb

The illustrations for this book were created with pencils, ink, watercolor paints, and digital art tools.

Printed in China by RR Donnelley Asia Printing Solutions Ltd., Dongguan City, Guangdong Province

5 7 9 10 8 6

OUR UNIVERSE

OCEAN!
WAVES FOR ALL

BY Ocean (WITH STACY MCANULTY)

ILLUSTRATED BY Ocean (AND DAVID LITCHFIELD)

Henry Holt and Company ✳ New York

Dude, I am OCEAN.

You know my many names:
Atlantic, Pacific, Arctic,
Indian, Southern.

It's all excellent me.

My salt water flows across
the planet as one.

I'm freeee!

Earth is called the blue planet
because of my epic, deep water.
I swirl over 71 PERCENT of our world.

I have no flag. No nationality.
My waves are for all.

I'm OLDER than the air you dudes breathe.

I've been here for about **four billion years.**

Most of my salty H_2O formed as baby Earth began chillin'.

As in, COOLING off.

For millions
of years, I was
cruising solo.

Then came Land.

Life on Earth began in my
epic waters. Way small at first.
Like, microscopic, man.

Single-celled
organisms

Bacteria

Algae

But life grows, changes,
and gets totally interesting.

Jellyfish

Fish

Multi-celled
organisms

Plant
Life

And like a boss, I hold some righteous records.

Home to Earth's . . .

Biggest animal. The blue whale dwarfs any dinosaur.

Longest mountain range. Meet the Mid-Ocean Ridge.

Largest living structure. The Great Barrier Reef.
This beauty can be seen from Moon. Far out!

I'm rolling in riches like gold, oil, silver, and even diamonds.

I don't need pavement to be the ultimate highway. More than 50,000 merchant ships can travel my waves on a single day.

I deliver food, clothes, toys, books, surfboards, and **everything** you dudes need.

I'm a deep, layered soul.

Sunlight Zone
(epipelagic)
0–200 meters (0–656 feet)

Midnight Zone
(bathypelagic)
1,000–4,000 m (3,281–13,123 ft)

Trenches
(hadalpelagic zone)
6,000 m+ (19,685 ft+)

My deepest spot, at 11,030 meters
(36,188 feet), is in the Mariana Trench.
I could swallow Mount Everest.

Twilight Zone
(mesopelagic)
200–1,000 m (656–3,281 ft)

Abyss
(abyssalpelagic zone)
4,000–6,000 m (13,123–19,685 ft)

Moon controls my tides.

High and Low.

Twice a day.

Harmony.

And I keep Earth's climate just right. At least, I try to.

I am the ultimate friend. Your bro.

Without me, there's no animals, no plants. No you.

I want people to know me.
You dudes have better
pictures of Mars
than of my bottom.
Chaa, it's true.

And more humans have visited
OUTER SPACE than my deepest spots.
Awesome for outer space. BUMMER for me.

Ninety percent of my waters are
completely dark, cold, and yet totally Rad.

Come explore my secrets.

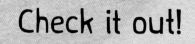

Check it out!

tube worms

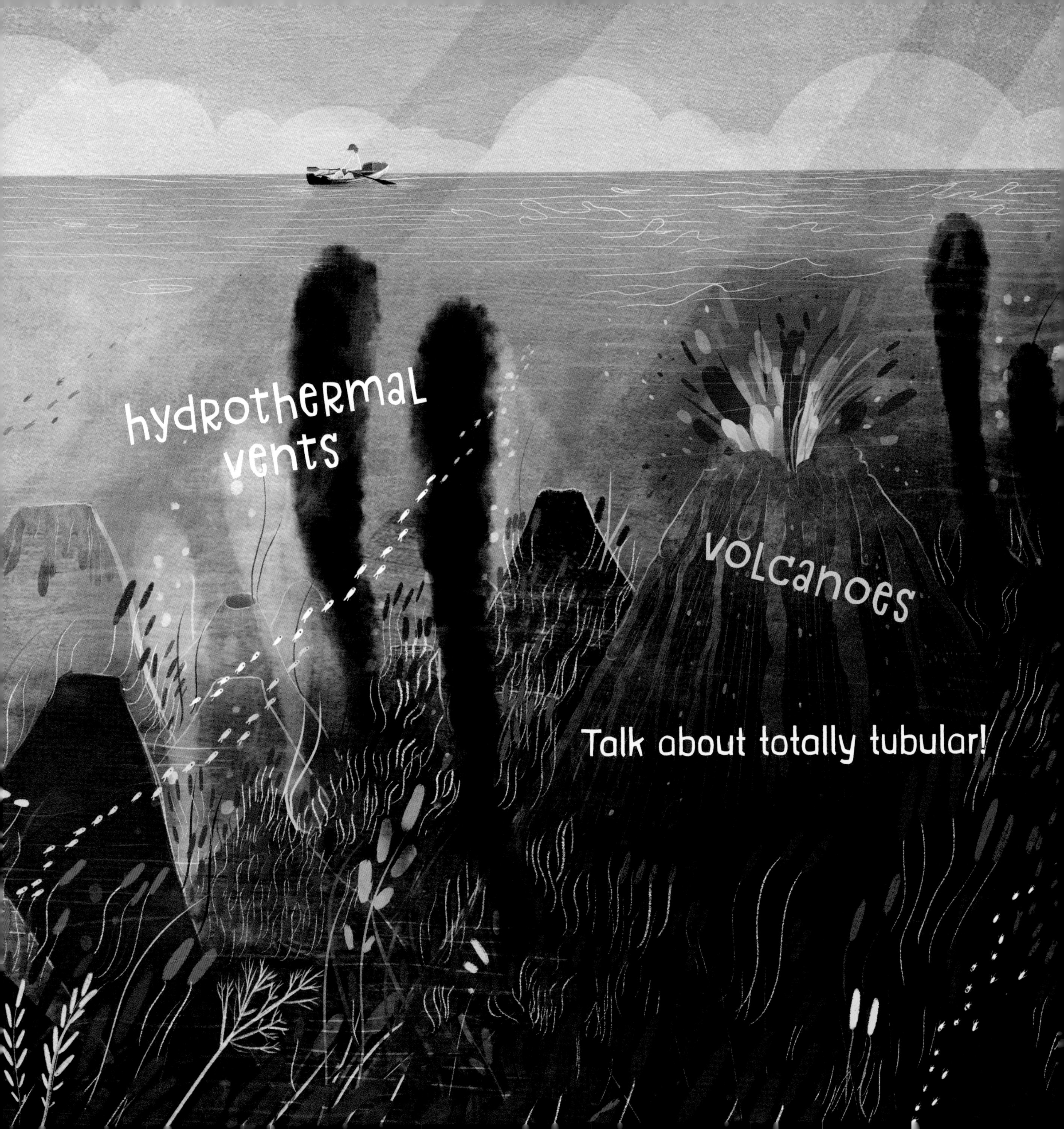

Talk about totally tubular!

Sad news, dudes. I'm facing
a major WIPEOUT.

Whole islands of plastic and
garbage float in my waters.
Whoa! Not cool.

Some creatures are struggling to survive. Overfishing is a major bummer.

Glaciers and icebergs are melting superfast. Too fast.

But together we can get back in the ZONE.

Let's find that
sweet balance.

I am your neighbor. Your friend.
Your past and your future.

Dude, I am
OCEAN.

Dear Thalassophile (that means *Ocean Lover*),

What would Earth be without Ocean? It certainly wouldn't be the generous home planet we've come to rely on. Water (and Ocean) are essential to life on Earth. Not only does Ocean provide half the oxygen in our atmosphere and regulate Earth's temperature, but without Ocean, swimming, surfing, and sailing would all be less enjoyable on land.

And even though Ocean covers 71 percent of our planet, we don't know much about him. There are secrets beneath the waves waiting for scientists—and future scientists—to discover. So much to dive into!

A splish and a splash,

Stacy McAnulty

Author, dude, and beachcomber

P.S. I've made every attempt to bring you accurate and fun information, but humans are learning more and more about Earth and Ocean all the time! I hope we all continue to learn and grow with science. (Yay, science!)

One vs. Five (or Four)

There's truly one global Ocean. Ocean is not divided by fences, walls, or land. However, humans have labeled Ocean as five (or four) separate bodies of water: Atlantic, Pacific, Arctic, Indian, and Southern (the "new" fifth Ocean). The separation is illustrated on maps and globes but cannot be seen on our actual planet.

Ocean by the Numbers

Ocean covers 71 percent of Earth's surface.

More than 80 percent of Ocean is unexplored.

On average, Ocean is 2.3 miles deep.

Challenger Deep in the Mariana Trench is 6.9 miles below sea level and is the deepest location on the planet.

The blue whale can grow to 98 feet long and 150 tons, making it the largest animal in Ocean (and on Earth).

The Mid-Ocean Ridge is the longest mountain range on Earth, at 40,389 miles.

The floor of the Atlantic Ocean widens by 0.5 inch to 4 inches per year.

The Great Barrier Reef is 135,000 square miles, which is bigger than the state of New Mexico.

Would You Rather . . . with Ocean

Let's play a game with our bro, Ocean.

Question 1: Would you rather be liquid or frozen solid?

Ocean: Solid, liquid, gas. Dude, how can I pick just one state of matter? It's not like picking a state of mind—if that was the question, I'd pick *chill*. I dig being both solid and liquid. About 15 percent of me is covered by sea ice for at least part of the year. Fresh water turns to ice at 32 degrees Fahrenheit. Salt water like me needs to be a chilly 28.4 degrees Fahrenheit.

Question 2: Would you rather swim with a whale or a shark?

Ocean: I appreciate all the creatures that swim in my excellent waters—from the 90 species of whales, dolphins, and porpoises to the 500-plus kinds of sharks. Even the smallest plankton are totally rad. Fish, mammals, reptiles, and birds all call my waters home. I'd never choose among them. Now, plastics on the other hand . . . keep plastics out of my waves.

Question 3: Would you rather eat only tacos or only pizza?

Ocean: Dude, I don't consume human food, and neither do my plethora of species. You can eat all the tacos and pizza you want. Just don't share it with seabirds or fish or any other nonhuman. I'm already a perfect ecosystem supplying food and harmony to creatures big and small. Radical.

Ocean: My turn. Would you rather live on a planet with healthy H_2O or a sick sea? It's a trick question, dude. Earth needs a healthy Ocean for peace and prosperity. Read on to learn how you can keep me happy and healthy.

How to Be a Friend to Ocean

1. Reduce your plastics. Islands of plastic float in Ocean. Switching to reusable water bottles and shopping bags can cut down on plastics in our environment.

2. Recycle. Sort through your trash and put recyclables in the right bins. If our used bottles, cans, and paper are headed to the recycling center, they're less likely to end up in Ocean's beautiful blue waves.

3. Conserve water. Even if you live a thousand miles from a beach, your wastewater can still make it to Ocean. Turn off the water while you brush your teeth, try short showers instead of baths, and fix leaky toilets.

4. Clean up. You can volunteer to clean up beaches in your area. And never throw items overboard or leave trash on the beach.

5. Buy and eat sustainable seafood. Fish is yummy and healthy, but overfishing can be a major problem. Eat only seafood that is caught in a way that won't hurt the fish population. You can find out which seafood is sustainable here: oceana.org/living-blue /sustainable-seafood-guide.

6. Use less energy overall. Turn off the lights, unplug the computer, walk instead of riding in the car. All these small ways can cut down on pollution that hurts Ocean and Earth.

7. Be careful with chemicals. Anything that goes down our sinks may end up in Ocean. Read labels on how to dispose of hazardous materials properly.

8. Write a letter. Share what you know with friends and write to lawmakers and tell them you care about Ocean's health.

Sources

Encyclopaedia Britannica, s.v. "Blue whale." Oct. 5, 2018. britannica.com/animal/blue-whale.

——, s.v. "Mid-Atlantic Ridge." April 15, 2010. britannica.com/place/Mid-Atlantic-Ridge.

——, s.v. "Ocean." By Alyn C. Duxbury and Claudia Cenedese. Feb. 20, 2019. britannica.com/science/ocean.

National Geographic. "10 Things You Can Do to Save the Ocean." April 27, 2010. nationalgeographic.com/environment/oceans/take-action/10-things-you-can-do-to-save-the-ocean/.

National Oceanic and Atmospheric Administration. "Can the Ocean Freeze?" National Ocean Service. Aug. 1, 2018. oceanservice.noaa.gov/facts/oceanfreeze.html.

——. "How Can You Help Our Oceans?" National Ocean Service. Accessed March 10, 2019. oceanservice.noaa.gov/ocean/help-our-ocean.html.

——. "How Deep Is the Ocean?" National Ocean Service. June 25, 2018. oceanservice.noaa.gov/facts/oceandepth.html.

——. "How Much of the Ocean Have We Explored?" National Ocean Service. July 11, 2018. oceanservice.noaa.gov/facts/exploration.html.

——. "What Is the Longest Mountain Range on Earth?" National Ocean Service. June 25, 2018. oceanservice.noaa.gov/facts/midoceanridge.html.

Oceana. "10 Things You Can Do to Save the Oceans." Accessed March 10, 2019. oceana.org/living-blue/10-things-you-can-do.

Wilsdon, Christina. *Ultimate Oceanpedia.* Washington, DC: National Geographic Partners, 2016.